S.E. HINTON

S.E. HINTON

JOSEPH FRANKLIN AND ANTOINE WILSON

ROSEN
PUBLISHING®

New York

ALL ABOUT THE AUTHOR™

Published in 2016 by The Rosen Publishing Group, Inc.
29 East 21st Street, New York, NY 10010

Library of Congress Cataloging-in-Publication Data

Franklin, Joseph, 1987-
S. E. Hinton / Joseph Franklin and Antoine Wilson. -- First edition.
    pages cm. -- (All about the author)
Includes bibliographical references and index.
ISBN 978-1-4994-6266-1 (library bound)
1. Hinton, S. E.--Juvenile literature 2. Authors, American--20th century--Biography--Juvenile literature. 3. Young adult fiction--Authorship--Juvenile literature. I. Wilson, Antoine. II. Title.
PS3558.I548Z67 2016
813'.54--dc23
[B]
                                                    2015016515

Manufactured in China

CONTENTS

In 1965, a fifteen-year-old teenage girl from Tulsa, Oklahoma, had no clue she was about to revolutionize young adult fiction with a story she was writing. She started writing it simply because she, herself, wanted something new to read—something more realistic than the novels marketed toward teens at the time. Instead of the cliché stories about characters that lived happily ever after, S. E. Hinton wanted to reflect the real struggles that come with growing up. Two years later, *The Outsiders* was published, and "YA" (or, young adult) fiction was never the same.

The Outsiders spoke to the real issues young people face, and time has proven its value. S. E. Hinton became a sensation, and the book sold well. An April 2014 article in the *Dallas Morning News* crunched the numbers: "*The Outsiders* has sold more than 14 million copies and still sells more than 500,000 copies every year." Now that's staying power! But who was the shy teenage author who wrote one of the best-selling YA novels of all time?

The first thing you should know is that the "S. E." in S. E. Hinton stands for Susan Eloise, and Susan Eloise Hinton is a woman. Most readers assume that Hinton is a man when they read her books. After all, the main characters of all of her novels are male, as are the narrators. The action—which can get pretty violent—often revolves around boys fighting with other boys. The female characters are usually minor,

Shown here in 1982, S. E. Hinton changed the YA (or, "young adult") genre forever with her gritty portrayal of realistic—and often violent—scenes of teenage life.

especially in Hinton's earlier works. In fact, the decision to use Hinton's initials was made by her publishers, who didn't want to advertise the fact that the writer of these tough-boy stories was a young woman.

The second thing you should know is that Hinton is a private person. She's never been interested in the spotlight and likes to keep her personal life out of the public eye. Hinton was born in Tulsa, Oklahoma, on July 22, 1950. She also grew up there and lives there to this day. Her passions—which include horseback riding, reading, and writing—are the same as when she was a kid.

As simple as Hinton's life sounds, it's been rather remarkable. By the time she was in college, Hinton had become one of the most successful YA authors of all time. In the process, she started a new trend in YA literature, writing realistic and gritty books for teenagers that spoke to what it really felt like to be a teen. She followed *The Outsiders* with a series of four other successful novels. Four of these fives YA novels became hit films.

In later years, Hinton wrote two children's books, a novel for adults, and a collection of short stories. Her earliest works, however, remain her biggest hits and continue to speak to new generations of readers. This is because Hinton tapped into something timeless— what it feels like to be a teenager. That is what makes her such a remarkable author.

A LOT IN COMMON WITH HER CHARACTERS

CHAPTER ONE

Susan Eloise Hinton was just a sophomore in high school when she began

writing her break-
through novel *The
Outsiders*. Hinton had
written several novels
as a student at Will
Rogers High School
in Tulsa, Oklahoma.
In fact, Hinton had
been writing since the
third grade. However,
her stories before *The
Outsiders* were mostly
about cowboys and
horses. Hinton claims
she wrote these stories

2007, Hinton returned to Will
gers High School, the Tulsa,
ahoma, school where she
ote her most popular work, *The
tsiders*, when she was just a
phomore.

9

simply because she wanted new books to read. After running out of books in her school library, she started writing stories of her own.

WRITING HER BREAKTHROUGH NOVEL

It took S. E. Hinton a year and a half to write *The Outsiders*. She went through four complete drafts of the novel in that time. First, she wrote a forty-page draft of the novel. Then she reread the draft, rewriting parts and adding details. In *The Fourth Book of Junior Authors & Illustrators*, Hinton is quoted explaining, "I happily wrote *The Outsiders* over and over again, not knowing what I was doing." She enjoyed the freedom of being a beginner, and she was primarily trying to entertain herself.

Despite being a novice, Hinton seemed to have some literary ambitions in mind. Her friend's mother was a writer, and Hinton showed her the manuscript for *The Outsiders* when she felt that it was done. This scored Hinton the contact information for a literary agent in New York. The agent read the novel and liked it, selling the book to the second publisher he tried, Viking Press.

Getting a novel published is not usually easy, especially for an unknown teenage writer from Tulsa, Oklahoma. Then again, no one had seen

A plaque and photograph of a teenaged S. E. Hinton are prominently displayed in Will Rogers High School, the high school Hinton attended while writing *The Outsiders* as well as the basis for the school featured in the novel.

anything quite like *The Outsiders* before. Hinton wrote it because she felt that all the books written for kids her age were unrealistic. She had moved beyond cowboy-and-horses books in search of good teenage books, ones that mirrored her real-life problems. In a November 1981 interview with *Seventeen* magazine, Hinton explained, "I'd wanted to read books that showed teenagers outside the life of 'Mary Jane went to the prom.'" Hinton's response to this shortage of novels is telling about her personality: "When I couldn't find any [good teenage books], I decided to write one myself. I created a world with no adult authority figures, where kids lived by their own rules."

THE OUTSIDERS (1967)

The Outsiders deals with a subject familiar to any-body who went to a large high school: the rivalry between two groups of kids. In the novel, the rivals are the poor, scrappy Greasers and the rich, fancy Socs (short for "socials"). Such rival cliques exist in many high schools, and even though different schools have different names for their groups, the struggles are often similar. Although Hinton did not belong to either group at her school, she got to see firsthand the way the groups dealt with each

A WORLD WITHOUT ADULTS

The Outsiders—like most of Hinton's novels—is notable for its lack of adults. In Hinton's world, teenage kids live on their own, without supervision and without any rules. This world is no fun-filled fantasy, though. The kids must figure out their own rules the hard way. In a sense, this is where Hinton's gritty realism comes from. While most readers of her books will never see a knife fight in real life (much less participate in one), the books seem realistic. And while most readers of her books do have authority figures and rules to contend with, her books depict a heightened version of the typical teenage experience: rebelling against authority while trying to figure things out for yourself.

While writing *The Outsiders*, Hinton had difficulties of her own. Her father was diagnosed with a brain tumor during her sophomore year of high school. He died in her junior year around the time she was finishing the book. In an April 1967 article in the *Tulsa Daily World*, Hinton's mother was quoted saying, "Susie was very close to her father, and I noticed the sicker he became, the harder she worked." The loss of her father is one reason why the emotions in *The Outsiders* are so urgent. The fantasy of a world without adults can be a nightmare for those who are actually going through the death of a parent, and Hinton might have sensed that losing her father meant she would have to figure out life on her own. The theme of teenagers figuring things out on their own became dominant in all of Hinton's young adult novels.

other. Mainly, she felt angry about the way the Socs treated the Greasers, driving by and yelling at them, or worse. She reacted to the situation in her own way, by writing about it. In an October 1967 *Seventeen* article, Hinton explained, "It was the cold-blooded beating of a friend of mine that gave me the idea of writing a book."

While the inspiration to write *The Outsiders* came from the world around her, Hinton did not just write the story of what happened in her school. She did

In this promotional still from the 1983 film adaptation of *The Outsiders*, the actors who played the Greasers, the rougher, tougher clique from the fictional high school portrayed in Hinton's most popular novel, are shown.

what many great writers do. She took the raw material of life, combined it with imagination and hard work, and made a fictional story out of it.

Hinton approached the conflict between the Greasers and the Socs through the interaction of her central characters. Some writers like to come up with a story or plot first, and then fill in character details along the way. Hinton's process is to start with characters and discover the plot later. Sometimes she will fill pages upon pages exploring the details of a single character, even a relatively minor one. As a result, she often knows a great deal about her characters—especially their motivations.

A Curious Choice of Narrators

Ponyboy Curtis was the first of Hinton's now-famous narrators. With him, Hinton began a tradition that has raised many questions; most of her characters are boys, including her narrators. Furthermore, she tends to write in the first person, using an "I" narrator to tell her stories. Many readers wonder, "Where are the girls?" Hinton has tried to explain herself several times over the years.

For one, Hinton herself was a tomboy growing up. Furthermore, when she was a teenager, the women's liberation movement had not taken off yet. The world of girls was more limited, and Hinton felt that if she wrote books from the point of view of a girl, people would not believe her stories. So she used a male narrator instead.

This decision turned out to be smart in terms of book sales. At the time, publishers felt that girls would read books marketed toward boys, but few boys would choose to read "girls'" books. That's also why Hinton's publisher decided that Susan Eloise Hinton should go by S. E. Hinton. Then, people would not know whether she was a man or a woman. Most readers, of course, assumed she was a man, and she received plenty of fan letters addressed to "Mr. Hinton."

REACTIONS TO HINTON'S FIRST BOOK

Now that *The Outsiders* is such a classic, it's easy to assume the book started flying off the shelves as soon as it was published. That wasn't the case. Sales were slow at first, but word of mouth helped slowly boost sales. Apparently, Hinton had not just written the book she wanted to read, but a book that countless other kids wanted to read, too. She had tapped into a whole new generation of readers, young people who had been waiting for a writer to come along and tell stories in their words from their perspective. She had quietly revolutionized young adult publishing by writing about what it really felt like to be a teenager.

Reviews for the book were mostly positive. Some reviewers criticized the novel for being overly sentimental or for having a plot that seemed overly convenient. Some readers felt that certain events in the book, rather than building upon previous events, seemed forced or out of place. For instance, the church fire that helps propel the book toward its conclusion was jarring to some. The presence of trapped children in the burning church—which, one chapter prior had been Ponyboy and Johnny's empty hideout—did not seem realistic. To some critics, it felt as if the schoolchildren were added simply so Ponyboy and Johnny could do something heroic. Others commented that the book was full of clichés. However, the book was sincere, and most critics recognized that Hinton's approach to class differences in the Greaser-Soc rivalry as well as Ponyboy's earnest tone would have a moving effect on young audiences.

Most reviewers were impressed by what this teenage wonder was able to write. In the *Atlantic Monthly*, writer Nat Hentoff praised Hinton's authenticity and energy, stating that she had "an astute ear and a lively sense of the restless rhythms of the

In this scene from the movie adaptation of *The Outsiders*, Ponyboy Curtis (as portrayed by C. Thomas Howell) speaks to one of the "Socs," Cherry Valance (played by Diane Lane). Ponyboy Curtis has remained one of S. E. Hinton's most popular narrators for generations.

young." In the *New York Times Book Review*, Thomas Fleming set aside the fact that Hinton was a teenager and wrote, "By almost any standard, Miss Hinton's performance is impressive." Yet, the best reactions came from the fans. Fans overwhelmingly connected with the characters in *The Outsiders* and praised Hinton for accurately depicting their struggles. Fan mail poured in, encouraging Hinton to keep writing.

By the time she was seventeen, S. E. Hinton was a success. She was in her freshman year of college at the University of Tulsa. She was able to pay for part of her education with royalties from her book. But being a teenage author

VIOLENCE IN *THE OUTSIDERS*

When *The Outsiders* began to get a lot of attention, some adults objected to the amount of violence that was portrayed in the book. Others complained that the book was sensationalist, or written just to create a scandal and make some money. Some even suggested that the book was not written by a real teenager and that Hinton's back story was a marketing ploy. They complained that reading the book would make teenagers more aggressive or expose readers to violence that they weren't ready to deal with. Hinton's refreshing response is still applicable today. In the August 27, 1967, edition of the *New York Times Book Review*, Hinton commented, "Adults who let small children watch hours of violence...on TV, scream their heads off when a book written for children contains a fist fight."

Hinton's book made many adults feel threated, if only because it didn't contain the typical themes they expected from a young adult novel. But Hinton wasn't interested in writing about following the rules and finding happiness; she wrote about dealing with the stress of being a teenager in a world without obvious rules or reliable adult guidance. Despite some adults' objections, the book was a commercial and critical success.

They grew up on the outside of society.
They weren't looking for a fight.
They were looking to belong.

ZOETROPE STUDIOS

FRANCIS FORD COPPOLA
PRESENTS

The Outsiders

S.E. Hinton's classic novel about youth.

Although the book's violence caused an uproar among many parents,
The Outsiders became a classic. Fifteen years after the novel hit the shelves,
a film adaptation was underway. It became a box office success.

was not all glamour and glory. In 1981, Hinton would tell *Seventeen* magazine that people who did not know her treated her as if she was "stuck-up." She explained, "I had always been a smart-alecky kid, but after the book was published, I knew I had to change, or else people would think success was going to my head. So I became quiet; but people saw that as being stuck-up, too." Whether she liked it or not, her book was a publishing phenomenon, and Hinton was famous. With publication, payment, and fame came the pressure of being a professional author, from whom something great was now expected.

COLLEGE AND CONTINUED SUCCESS

With the success of *The Outsiders*, teenage tomboy Susie Hinton had suddenly become famous novelist S. E. Hinton. And with fame came many things Hinton never expected. Interviews, book tours, and young fans with endless questions all became a part of Hinton's life. She was a professional writer—no longer working alone on stories no one else would read. Everyone wanted to know what she would write next, including Hinton herself. She was ready to get started on another novel, but there was one problem: she couldn't write! The pressure Hinton felt trying to live up to the big expectations gave her a bad case of writer's block.

In a September 1985 interview with the *Wilson Library Bulletin*, Hinton shared, "Right off I had writer's block for years. I couldn't even write a letter. It was like everybody was waiting to see what this teenage wonder was going to do next. The next one had to be a masterpiece." Hinton had written *The Outsiders* in a vacuum: she simply let the story and its characters take her away into another world. Nobody expected anything from her. All this changed, though, after the publication of that novel.

COLLEGE YEARS AND MEETING HER HUSBAND

On top of the big expectations from her newfound success, Hinton was also now at college, where she was being exposed to a range of great literature. Suddenly, she was reading books she had never read before. As she read more and more great writers, she doubted her own ability. In an interview in the *University of Tulsa Annual*, Hinton said, "I read *The Outsiders* again when I was 20, and I thought it was the worst piece of trash I'd ever seen. I magnified all its faults."

At the University of Tulsa, Hinton majored in education and considered a career in teaching. Trying to become a teacher seemed logical at the time, as she had always enjoyed the company of kids. However, as part of her program, Hinton did some student teaching, and she started to think that maybe it was not the right career for her. She found it exhausting—both physically and emotionally. She found herself coming home from teaching and continuing to worry about the kids and their problems. She also grew depressed. She was a writer, after all, and yet she wasn't doing any writing. This was where David Inhofe came in.

Hinton and Inhofe met in a freshman biology class and started going out soon afterward. Inhofe (who would later become Hinton's husband) became concerned about Hinton's depression. He knew the solution. She had to write. Even though the best writing often comes from a writer who is inspired and feeling creative, nothing at all comes from a writer who isn't writing. Inhofe came up with a strategy to get his girlfriend writing again. She had to write two pages a day, simple as that. He knew that as long as she was writing, she wouldn't be depressed.

THAT WAS THEN, THIS IS NOW (1971)

Soon, Hinton got too busy working on her new book to be depressed. Even though she didn't feel confident while writing *That Was Then, This Is Now*, it was clear that she had grown from writing *The Outsiders*. She learned that discipline and good writing habits are big parts of the equation. In a talk at the Boston Public Library, Hinton said, "I was very careful with this book, and I wanted each sentence to be exactly right, and I'd just sweat out my two pages, and I'd put them in a stack." Then, with her work done for the day, she and Inhofe would go out.

It wasn't long before Hinton had a novel-sized manuscript ready to go to the publisher. She sent it off, and it was accepted immediately. Not only that, but the editors didn't ask her to do any major rewrites. This, as much as anything, is proof of the discipline with which she approached writing those two pages every day.

That Was Then… is narrated by Bryon Douglas, who, in many ways, is similar to Ponyboy. He's not a bad kid; he's just caught up in bad circumstances. One source of his trouble is Mark Jennings, his best friend. Mark lives with Bryon and Bryon's mother because he's an orphan; his parents killed each other in a fight. Bryon's mother is in the hospital, so the boys basically have the house to themselves. Once again, Hinton had created a world in which kids are left alone to learn difficult life lessons without the help of their parents.

While *The Outsiders* was concerned with the loss of innocence, *That Was Then…* took a different

Released in 1971 as a novel and in 1985 as a film adaption, *That Was Then, This Is Now* was S. E. Hinton's successful follow-up to her debut work, *The Outsiders*. In *That Was Then...*, Hinton explored how a friendship can change over time as two people grow apart.

approach to the way people change over time. Instead of focusing on one character's attempt to keep his innocence in a topsy-turvy world, Hinton's second novel looked at how Bryon and Mark's friendship changes over time. Different approaches to this theme would appear again in Hinton's later novels.

After finishing *That Was Then...*, Hinton was exhausted and needed a break. She and Inhofe got married in September 1970 and vacationed in Europe.

CROSSOVER BETWEEN *THAT WAS THEN...* AND *THE OUTSIDERS*

One notable feature of S. E. Hinton's young adult novels that fans love is continuity. Certain plot elements—including key characters, events, and setting—recur in several of Hinton's works. This first occurs in *That Was Then, This is Now*. The setting in Hinton's second novel was the same as in *The Outsiders*. Ponyboy Curtis even makes an appearance in *That Was Then...*, sparking a fight that lands Mark in a hospital emergency room. Perhaps Hinton liked Ponyboy too much to let him go. Maybe she just wanted to connect this novel to *The Outsiders* to let careful readers know that she was writing about the same world she'd created in the first book. Either way, Ponyboy came back, and fans of *The Outsiders* got excited about seeing him from another point of view. The view is especially interesting because Bryon doesn't like Ponyboy. Later novels would also occur in the same town with connections between new characters and those of Hinton's earlier works.

Bryon Douglas (shown here is Craig Sheffer's portrayal of the character in the film adaptation of *That Was Then, This Is Now*) was the narrator of Hinton's second novel. He lived in the same fictional town from Hinton's first novel, *The Outsiders*.

ONE-HIT WONDER?

Whether or not reviewers liked Hinton's second novel, they uniformly noticed the discipline Hinton had put into writing it. The structure of *That Was Then...* was more controlled, and the plot seemed better planned than in *The Outsiders*. Some critics appreciated that her style was maturing, while others missed the young, raw energy of *The Outsiders*. The latter group thought *That Was Then...* was too controlled, too emotionally cool.

Michael Cart, writing in the *New York Times Book Review*, praised Hinton's handling of theme in the book: "The phrase 'if only' is perhaps the most bittersweet in the language, and Miss Hinton uses it skillfully to underline her theme: growth can be a dangerous process." He wrote that *That Was Then...* was "a mature, disciplined novel, which excites a response in the reader. Whatever its faults, the book will be hard to forget."

Hinton continued her string of awards with the publication of *That Was Then, This Is Now.* What started as the book Hinton needed to write simply to keep going became her next hit. Now no one could say she was just a one-hit wonder. No one could dismiss *The Outsiders* as a fluke or a publicity scheme. S. E. Hinton was to be taken seriously.

DEPARTURE AND RETURN TO FORM

In between writing *The Outsiders* and *That Was Then, This Is Now*, Hinton had written a short story called *"Rumble Fish."* She published it in a magazine called *Nimrod*, a supplement to the *University of Tulsa Alumni Magazine*. This short story Hinton initially wrote had most of the elements that ended up in her third full-length book, *Rumble Fish*.

Hinton got the idea for the story from a picture she had cut out of a magazine around 1967. The picture was of a boy and a motorcycle. Something about the image fascinated Hinton. By the time *Rumble Fish* was published, she couldn't even remember what magazine it had come from. Apparently, she kept that magazine clip-out for years to come.

THE CHALLENGE OF
CRAFTING *RUMBLE FISH*

Having a complete short story in hand would seem to make writing the novel easier than starting from scratch. After all, Hinton only had to expand the short story, right? If things were only that simple. Hinton's major problem in writing her third book was trying to decide on her narrator. The short story moved around from character to character, but for the novel Hinton wanted a single character to tell the story. Apparently, she wrote an entire draft of the novel, from page one to the end, with the straight-laced character Steve as the narrator. It wasn't good enough for her. As Hinton explained, "I already had the book done, and I read it over and just couldn't stand it. It was too easy; he was too intelligent, he was too articulate, too observant."

Hinton wanted a challenge. She got the idea to have the troubled Rusty-James tell the story instead of the well-spoken Steve. In Rusty-James, she was trying to create a character who could not explain everything about himself. This was a challenge because, unlike the narrators of her previous books, Ponyboy and Bryon, this

n director Francis Ford Coppola's film adaptation of *Rumble Fish* (1983), actor Matt Dillon shown here) portrayed Rusty-James. In contrast to Hinton's previous narrators, Rusty-ames was not well-spoken and could not always verbalize what he thought or felt.

narrator wasn't as good at expressing himself or as aware of his emotions. Hinton wanted the novel to be about the way Rusty-James identifies with his older brother Motorcycle Boy (a legendary street gang fighter) without being able to understand him.

One thing readers of *Rumble Fish* notice is its interesting structure. The first chapter and the final chapter both happen after the main plot has already occurred. Rusty-James runs into his old friend Steve down by the beach. A lot has happened since they last saw each other, and seeing Steve reminds Rusty-James of the story that makes up the bulk of the novel. It's as if Hinton took the main theme of *That Was Then, This Is Now* (friends whose lives move in different directions) and used it to tell another story.

Framing the plot as Hinton did was a bold move. She used what is called a flashback narrative, one in which part of the story's end comes first followed by the events that led up to it. Hinton ran the risk that some readers would get confused by the shift in time, but in *Rumble Fish*, that risk paid off. It gave Hinton the freedom to share the ending before readers knew the whole story. As a result, Hinton could focus on how things happen rather than what is going to happen.

HINTON ON THE WRITER'S LIFE

The life of a writer can seem glamorous to some, but Hinton's life has always been pretty simple. On her own website, Hinton puts it bluntly: "A writer's life is not very exciting; usually you're alone in a room with your tools—paper, pen, imagination." In a Q&A for the Random House publishing website, she noted how her writing habits change with her day-to-day demands. She states, "I keep changing my methods, working around other things in my life. *That Was Then, This Is Now* was written in the two-pages-a-day method. *Rumble Fish* was written on Thursday nights, because that was when my husband played poker." She goes on to note that her "one technique throughout is to be flexible about time and seize it when [she] can."

Hinton's husband, David Inhofe, has remained a positive force in her writing. In a July 1982 interview for the *Los Angeles Times*, Hinton said, "I like to have [David] read what I'm working on, but only to tell me that he likes it. I don't want anybody criticizing my work while I'm doing it. But every once in a while he makes some good suggestions." The artistic process is fragile, and having someone close who can give positive reinforcement can be very helpful. Criticism at the wrong time can send writers into a panic. Hinton would later adapt her writer's life to motherhood after the birth of her son, Nicholas. Nicholas would become a strong influence when Hinton took a shot at writing children's books for a younger audience.

RESPONSE TO HER THIRD NOVEL

The reviews of *Rumble Fish* were mixed, not because people's reactions were tame or luke-warm, but because some reviewers loved the book and others didn't like it at all. The opinions ranged from a *Publishers Weekly* review claiming that Hinton was a "brilliant novelist" to a *Kirkus* review that said that Hinton "seems to have no more of a future, or even a present, than Rusty-James has."

Jane Powell, in the April 2, 1976, *Times Literary Supplement*, called the book "a disappointment." Her reasons are interesting and relate to Rusty-James's inability to fully understand his situation. Powell wrote, "The earlier two books [*The Outsiders* and *That Was Then...*] also deal with the American delinquent scene, but in both, the central character has an intelligence and sensitivity which set him apart from his peers... [Rusty-James] involves himself in situations largely out of loyalty to others and at the end... is left wiser and sadder."

On the other hand, Margery Fisher, in her May 1976 review published in the magazine *Growing Point*, called *Rumble Fish* "a book as uncompromising in its view of life as it is disciplined in form... Of the three striking books by this young author, *Rumble Fish* seems the most carefully structured and the most probing." Fisher seemed to like exactly what Powell complained about. She appreciated the way Hinton showed life without watering down the bad parts.

Why the difference of opinion? Author Jay Daly, in his critical book about Hinton's work, *Presenting S. E. Hinton* (1989), said:

> The success or failure of [*Rumble Fish*] rests with its ability to bring the reader into contact, not so much with the motivations of the characters or the answers to their particular problems, but with the mythic sense of life itself, with the element of mystery for which there are no answers but belief.

Readers who tapped into that "element of mystery" were excited to see Hinton moving in new, more ambitious directions. Readers who were looking for more of the same were disappointed by Hinton's desire to tackle larger questions.

Regardless of the critics' reactions, *Rumble Fish* won many awards, among them an American Library Association Best Books for Young Adults citation in 1975. Hinton calls *Rumble Fish* her most "literary" book. She says it is the easiest to read but the hardest to understand. Of all of her books,

it is the one she most recom-
mended her readers revisit
when they're older.

A RETURN TO FORM WITH *TEX*

Although it was one of
the most difficult to write,
Hinton's 1979 novel *Tex*
became the crowning
achievement of Hinton's
work to date. In order to
write it, Hinton set a new
challenge for herself: to
write a book focused on
relationships in which the
events seemed natural
and realistic and in which
the central character (Tex
McCormick) becomes
more mature by the end
of the book.

In contrast to Rusty-
James, the narrator of
Rumble Fish who lacked
self-awareness, Hinton
created a more typical

Matt Dillon's portrayal of the titular character in the 1982 film adaptation of *Tex* earned praise from film critics and helped launch his successful acting career. Above he is shown flanked by actors Emilio Estevez and Meg Tilly, who also starred in the film.

Hinton narrator, albeit a more mature one than Ponyboy or Bryon. In a press release from her publisher, Hinton called Tex McCormick "the most childlike character I've ever done, but the one who makes the greatest strides toward maturity. I have to admit he's a favorite child." Unlike Ponyboy, who tended to think like the young Hinton, Tex McCormick is a fully fleshed-out character who is significantly different from Hinton. Creating such a character is a challenge for any writer, and Hinton combined it with the desire to make a novel that seemed realistic and smooth, and which didn't rely on flashy plot events to keep readers engaged.

It's not surprising that, of all her novels, *Tex* took Hinton the longest to write. She spent three and a half years just figuring out the events that would drive the plot. But this time, she was not suffering from writer's block, as she had with *That Was Then, This Is Now*. Instead, Hinton wanted to take her time to construct *Tex* very carefully so it would seem smooth, natural, and unforced.

Hinton had the luxury of time as well as the maturity to know how to use it well. In an interview published in the 1983–84 *University of Tulsa Annual*, Hinton talked about her writing process: "Getting from point A to Z is just so hard for me,

A FAMILIAR NARRATIVE WORLD

The world of *Tex* is one familiar to any Hinton fan: teenage boys trying to get by without parents around. Fourteen-year-old Tex McCormick lives with his brother, Mason. Their mother is dead, and their father is traveling on the rodeo circuit, leaving the boys on their own. Because they need money, Mason decides to sell off their horses—including Tex's horse, Negrito—to pay the bills. Tex is enraged by Mason's decision to sell the horses, in part because he doesn't yet understand adult responsibilities such as paying bills. Much of the story focuses on Tex and Mason's relationship and how it changes as the two brothers grow apart.

Careful readers of *That Was Then, This Is Now* recognized *The Outsiders'* Ponyboy Curtis when he reappeared in that novel, but it takes a really sharp eye to spot the reappearance of an old Hinton character in *Tex*. The hitchhiker who kidnaps Mason and Tex is actually Mark from *That Was Then, This Is Now*, and he has just busted out of jail.

and I get off on tangents and write 50 pages on a minor character. So I think, this isn't going to be the direction I thought, and I tear it up. What's going to happen next? I need to get *Tex* from there over here, but how do I do that?" Hinton

Shown here is S. E. Hinton with actor Matt Dillon, who portrayed the character Tex McCormick in the film adaptation of Hinton's novel *Tex*. The novel was widely recognized as one of Hinton's best works, and it became the first Hinton book to be turned into a movie.

shows here that writing a novel can be a difficult and frustrating process, with lots of false starts and dead ends.

Reviewers immediately recognized that *Tex* was an achievement for Hinton and that her craft had continued to improve over the years. Marilyn Kaye, in a November 1979 *School Library Journal* review, stated that, "Hinton's style has matured since she exploded onto the young adult (YA) scene in 1967." She went on to say that Hinton's "raw energy" had not been "tamed," but rather, "cultivated." In other words, Hinton had managed to keep her original vision while also developing her craft. Margery Fisher, in the May 1980 issue of *Growing Point*, praised Hinton's ability to create the "illusion of reality," an important element in any work of fiction. There is nothing out of place to distract the reader from Tex's story.

In addition to praise from critics, *Tex* also received its fair share of awards, highlighting its standing among the best of Hinton's books. These included an American Library Association Best Books for Young Adults citation as well as a *School Library Journal* Best Books of the Year citation the year it came out.

HINTON'S WORLD HITS THE BIG SCREEN

The 1980s would become an important decade for S. E. Hinton in a new medium: film. Her most recently published novel at the time, *Tex* (1979), was the first Hinton book adapted for the big screen. The rights to make the movie were bought by Disney Studios, which made Hinton a little uncomfortable. She was familiar with other Disney movies and was worried that the company would try to change her story to make it more kid-friendly, which wouldn't be true to the book. However, Hinton got lucky with *Tex*. As a matter of fact, she had luck with the film adaptations of all her novels.

CHAPTER FOUR

TEX

From Walt Disney Productions

Seen here is the promotional poster for the film adaptation of *Tex*. Hinton worried that Disney would make the movie version too kid-friendly, but the production company kept true to the novel, earning a PG rating instead of the typical G that most Disney films received.

FIRST UP, *TEX*

Tex, the movie, was released in 1982. Its screenplay was written by director Tim Hunter and writer Charlie Haas. Hunter came to the project with an idea of what makes an S. E. Hinton novel special, and he understood that the strength of her novels should not be lost in the film version. In a March 1983 *New York Times* article, he said, "Susie deals with many of the social problems that other young adult writers confront, but in her books those problems are woven into the fabric of a realistic story. She never preaches or moralizes." Hunter's movie remained true to the basic plot of the book. He made sure any differences stayed in line with Tex's character in the novel.

The movie was shot in Tulsa, and Hinton was there for the shoot. Some novelists get involved with the movie adaptations of their books, and some leave everything in the hands of the moviemakers. Hinton chose to work closely with Tim Hunter, finding good locations to shoot and interacting with the actors.

The movie was a lucky break for actor Matt Dillon. (Dillon went on to become a major movie star, later appearing in dozens of Hollywood blockbusters). Hinton, in an article from the April 1983 issue of *American Film* magazine, recalled her first

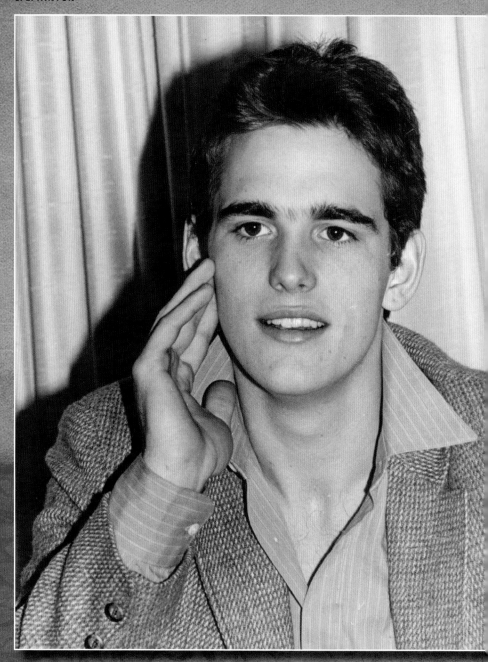

Actor Matt Dillon appears before the Hollywood Foreign Press at a December 1982 meeting at the Beverly Hilton Hotel to discuss the movie *Tex*. Dillon's role in the film would help launch his successful acting career.

impression of Dillon. "Tex is a sweet little unworldly cowboy, and here was this guy who said, 'Like, man,' and told me *Rumble Fish* was his favorite book. When I get a letter from a kid who says *Rumble Fish* is his favorite book, he's usually in a reformatory [that is, a juvenile detention center]." It took her a little while to warm up to Dillon, but once they hit it off, they got along really well. As Hinton said, "All of a sudden, I thought, I made this kid up; I wrote this kid. He was exactly the kid I was writing about and for—really bright, doesn't fit into the system, has possibilities beyond the obvious." Dillon went on to play major roles in movie versions of *The Outsiders* (released in March 1983) and *Rumble Fish* (released in October 1983), as well.

Hinton made her own first foray into acting with *Tex*. She makes a brief cameo in the movie, playing a role she knew well from her college years when she was majoring in education: a teacher. And she's not the only Hinton "family" member to appear in the movie. Her horse, Toyota, played the role of Tex's horse, Negrito.

HINTON MEETS COPPOLA

The next film adaptation of one of Hinton's books was *The Outsiders*, which was directed by Francis

Ford Coppola and written by Kathleen Knutson Howell. How *The Outsiders* got made into a movie is an interesting story. In March 1980, several months before anyone approached Hinton with the idea to make *Tex* into a movie, some kids from the Lone Star School in Fresno, California, wrote a letter to the famous director Francis Ford Coppola asking him to consider making *The Outsiders* into a movie.

Fortunately for them, the kids sent the letter to the wrong address. They sent it to Paramount Pictures, which was the right studio, but instead of sending it to the production offices in Hollywood, they sent the letter to the corporate headquarters in New York City. The corporate headquarters was where all of the business affairs of the studio went on, not where people actually made movies. However, Coppola happened to be in New York at the time, and since he didn't get much mail there, he read the letter personally. If the letter had gone to Hollywood, it probably would have ended up in a big pile of unread mail!

Coppola's reaction, producer Fred Roos said in a March 1983 *New York Times* article, was something along the lines of, "Look at that cute letter. I bet kids have a good idea of what should be a movie. Check it out, if you want to." So Roos decided to give *The Outsiders* a chance. He wasn't excited at first. He thought the book jacket was tacky, "like the book had been privately printed by some religious organization." However, he decided to read ten pages and see if the book was any good. He ended up reading it cover to cover in one sitting, and just like the students of Lone Star School, Roos thought it would make a great movie, too.

In the summer of 1980, Roos went to Oklahoma to talk to Hinton, and she agreed to sell Coppola the rights to make the movie. (A week later, Disney approached her about the rights to *Tex*.) In a December 1982 *Chicago Tribune* article, Hinton said that she had "never planned to sell the movie rights to [her] books. They mean so much to a lot of kids that [she] didn't want to see them messed up." But Hinton had seen *The Black Stallion*, adapted from Walter Farley's book by Coppola's studio, and she was pleased with the job they had done.

Still, Hinton wasn't sure about Coppola until they began working together. It was not until Coppola visited her in Tulsa—to show her how he was writing the screenplay—that she became totally convinced he could make the movie. Coppola showed her how he had broken down

Famous film director Francis Ford Coppola (*upper left*) gives direction to three of the actors between filming scenes for *The Outsiders*. Coppola would go on to direct the movie adaptation of *Rumble Fish* as well.

the book into passages of action and passages of introspection, and how he was using that breakdown to write the screenplay. She was impressed.

Coppola, for his part, was quoted in the aforementioned *Chicago Tribune* article saying, "When I met Susie, it was confirmed to me that she was not just a young people's novelist, but a real American novelist. For me a primary thing about her books is that the characters come across as very real. Her dialogue is memorable, and her prose is striking. Often a paragraph of descriptive prose sums up something essential and stays with you." Thus began a working relationship between Coppola and Hinton that would last for two movies.

Many novelists do not get actively involved in the movie adaptations of their books, but S. E. Hinton (*left*) was on set for three of the four films based on her novels. She developed a friendship with director Francis Ford Coppola (*right*), who directed two of those films.

Hinton got very involved with the making of *The Outsiders*, and she was a presence on the set. Among other things, Coppola depended on her as "a security blanket and expert on things 'southwestern,'" as one of the executives at Coppola's production company put it. She was paid as a consultant for her help. Not only that, but she continued her acting career with another cameo role. In *The Outsiders*, Hinton plays a nurse.

Before the movie came out, the high school students who suggested the movie got treated to a preview screening. The film's stars came and met the kids who made the film possible in the first place.

This movie is not as faithful to the book as *Tex* was. Part of the reason was Coppola's vision for the movie. As Jay Daly wrote in *Presenting S. E. Hinton*, "Coppola tried to expand the movie into something like myth, into a statement about youth and America, and unfortunately the continuity of the story got lost somewhere (probably on the cutting room floor)." Somewhere in the attempt to make the story more universal, the story itself got muddled. The movie has it fans, though, especially among people who have already read the book and know the story pretty well.

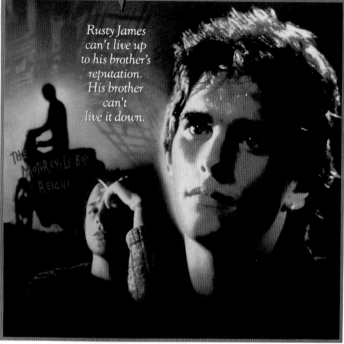

FRANCIS FORD COPPOLA
PRESENTS

rumble FISH

Rusty James can't live up to his brother's reputation. His brother can't live it down.

THE MOTORCYCLE BOY REIGNS

RUMBLE FISH

starring

MATT DILLON   MICKEY ROURKE
as Rusty James   as the Motorcycle Boy

VINCENT SPANO   DIANE LANE   DIANA SCARWID
NICOLAS CAGE   and   DENNIS HOPPER

Screenplay by

S. E. HINTON & FRANCIS COPPOLA

Based on the novel by   Music by   Executive Producer
S. E. HINTON   STEWART COPELAND   FRANCIS COPPOLA

Edited by   Production Designer   Director of Photography
BARRY MALKIN   DEAN TAVOULARIS   STEPHEN H. BURUM, A.S.C.

Produced by   Directed by
FRED ROOS   and   DOUG CLAYBOURNE   FRANCIS COPPOLA

From Zoetrope Studios

RESTRICTED
R

SEE IT THIS FALL AT SELECTED THEATRES

Almost immediately after they wrapped up filming *The Outsiders*, Coppola and Hinton teamed up again to turn *Rumble Fish* into a movie as well. For the third time in a row, Matt Dillon starred in a movie adaptation of one of Hinton's novels.

COPPOLA AND HINTON'S NEXT ENDEAVOR

Rumble Fish, the movie, grew out of the making of *The Outsiders*. Halfway through the filming of *The Outsiders*, Coppola, pleased with how things were going, asked Hinton if she had another novel he could make into a movie. She told him about *Rumble Fish*, and he proposed that they write the screenplay on their days off, Sundays. After *The Outsiders* was finished, they took a two-week break before starting work on *Rumble Fish*. In a March 1983 *New York Times* article, Hinton said that she laughed off Coppola's proposed plan as too much work, but acknowledged that she ended up following suit. Hinton focused on the dialogue, and Coppola focused on the visual images and structure. Hinton played a major role in the moviemaking process, and in no time, they had another movie.

Rumble Fish was released the same year as *The Outsiders* and starred Matt Dillon as Rusty-James. The film was shot in black and white to highlight Rusty-James's colorblindness. Coppola's vision paid off, and *Rumble Fish* the movie captured the mood and substance of its namesake novel. Hinton's acting career

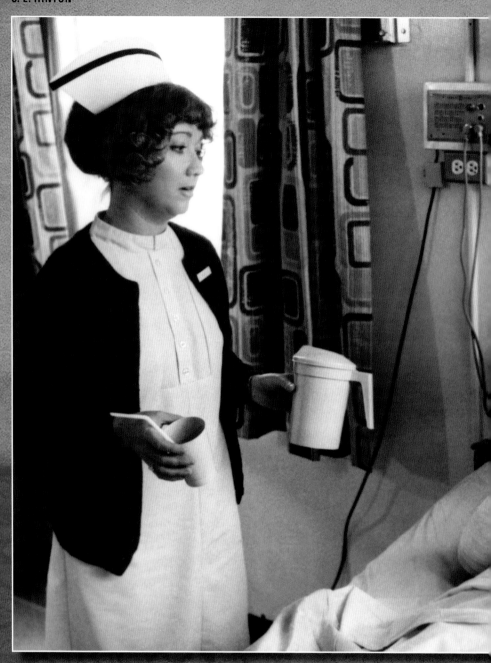

In addition to her active role in adapting her novels' storylines for the big screen, Hinton also made cameos in several of the movie versions of her books. Here she is shown as the nurse who tends to Dallas Winston (portrayed by Matt Dillon) in *The Outsiders* (1983).

continued with *Rumble Fish*. During the carnival-like city scene, Hinton had a cameo as a streetwalker.

HINTON'S FINAL FILM

Of the four films made from Hinton's novels, *That Was Then, This Is Now* (released in 1985) was the only one she was not involved with. She also did not appear in the movie. Emilio Estevez, the already well-known actor who had previously appeared in both *Tex* and *The Outsiders*, introduced his father, actor and producer Martin Sheen, to Hinton's novels. Sheen

HINTON ON HOLLYWOOD

In a March 20, 1983, article published in the *New York Times*, Hinton summed up her initial movie-making experiences. She said, "It's the first time I've ever felt at home in a group situation. I've never been a joiner. In Tulsa I have a reputation for being slightly eccentric. Even my close friends think I'm a little nutty. But with the movie people I was accepted instantly."

At the time of the article, Hinton had already completed the films *Tex* and *The Outsiders*, and initial work on *Rumble Fish* had already begun. Hinton was closely involved in the making of those first three films. She went on to say, "I really like the way people support each other on a movie set. One of the guys on the crew who had been in Vietnam told me that making a movie is the closest thing to being in a battle that you can find in civilian life. You get the same camaraderie." That camaraderie was something Hinton enjoyed a lot.

Hinton went on to explain that, as an author, she often felt a great deal of pressure to make her works perfect. However, when shooting a film, a whole team is responsible for the success or failure of the shoot. In Hinton's own words, "And there's one other nice thing about movies. There's always somebody else to blame. With a novel, you have to take all the blame yourself."

Despite her love of filmmaking, after Hinton's four extant novels at the time had been turned into movies, the author never took an active role in filmmaking again. Only years later, in 2009, would Hinton make a brief cameo in another film (not based on any of her works), *Legend of Billy Fail* (2009). Hinton played a school principal. In 2011, she would make an uncredited appearance as a diner patron in an episode of the television series *Supernatural*.

bought the rights to make the film, and Estevez went to work on the screenplay. The film, which starred Estevez as Mark Jennings, was released in 1985. Of all the films made from S. E. Hinton novels, *That Was Then...* was the least faithful to the book in terms of storyline. The book is set in the wild and confusing late 1960s, but the movie does not concern itself with the period as much, aiming for a timeless feeling. Also, the book's hard-hitting ending was softened for the film adaptation.

After the production of *That Was Then...*, Hinton would return to writing, the profession she loved.

ELIMINATION
POOL TOURNAMENT

OPEN CHALLENGE in ALL
CLASSES!! (see course for
Days & Details)

Emilio Estevez, who played Two-Bit in the movie version of *The Outsiders* and Johnny Collins in the movie *Tex*, starred as Mark Jennings alongside Craig Sheffer (who portrayed Bryon Douglas) in the film *That Was Then, This Is Now*.

Despite all of the glamour of movie-making—including the pleasures of working with actors such as Matt Dillon and with director Francis Ford Coppola—one gets the feeling that Hinton's Hollywood stint did not change her work ethic much. She simply returned to normal life in Tulsa and her typewriter.

CHAPTER FIVE

HINTON'S RETURN TO WRITING

There was quite a gap between the publication of Hinton's fourth novel *Tex* (1979) and her return to publishing nine years later with *Taming the Star Runner*. Hinton, of course, had kept herself busy with the movie adaptations of her first four books. In August 1983, she and her husband, David Inhofe, had also become parents to their son, Nicholas David Inhofe. But by the time *That Was Then, This Is Now* was in production, Hinton had been away from her writing long enough.

BECOMING A YA LEGEND

In 1987, a major critical study of Hinton's work by author Jay Daly was published.

Daly's book, *Presenting S. E. Hinton*, marked Hinton's serious recognition as a writer. It explored the themes, characters, and critical reactions to all of Hinton's books. Most important, *Presenting S. E. Hinton* took Hinton's books seriously and examined them as literature. Even though the books were best sellers and were frequently reviewed by major newspapers and magazines, no one had yet written a serious study of Hinton's work. This was a big deal and an honor to any writer—especially in the young adult (YA) genre.

Then, in 1988, Hinton received the first ever YASD/SLJ Margaret A. Edwards Award, which is given by the Young Adult Services Division of the American Library Association and by *School Library Journal*. This award recognizes more than just one book; it recognizes a lifetime of achievement. The fact that Hinton was chosen as the first recipient shows how important her books were to the field of young adult literature.

With the publication of *The Outsiders* in 1967, Hinton had just about single-handedly transformed the entire genre. She was among the first to begin to confront the real issues that teenagers faced. After proving she had staying power, Hinton's books influenced generations of readers and— perhaps just as important—generations of writers.

Hinton holds up a copy of *The Outsiders* at the 93rd Annual American Booksellers Association Convention and Trade Show in 1993. By the late 1980s, Hinton was a YA legend largely credited with helping create the genre with her groundbreaking work.

Before Daly's book, and before she received the Author Achievement Award, Hinton's reputation was already solid. For example, in a 1985 *Wilson Library Bulletin* article, Patty Campbell called S. E. Hinton a "walking YA legend," "the Queen of Young Adult Novel," and "the Grand Old Lady of YA Lit." But Daly's critical study and the YASD/SLJ Award made Hinton's standing official.

The question, of course, was whether or not Hinton would live up to the hype with her new book. Would she have trouble writing about teenagers as she became older? What effect would motherhood have on her books? Could Hinton, now a "Grand Old Lady," still write a convincing book about teenagers?

HINTON'S RETURN TO WRITING

Released in 1988, *Taming the Star Runner* differed from Hinton's first four novels in a significant way. This story was not narrated by the main character. Hinton's previous four novels were told in the first person from the perspectives of Ponyboy, Bryon, Rusty-James, and Tex, respectively. For example, in *The Outsiders*, the whole novel is constructed as a paper Ponyboy writes for his English class. In *Taming the Star Runner*, however, the narrator stands outside the action. Travis does not tell us his story himself. Instead of being written in the first person, the book is written in the third person, with Travis's thoughts and actions related by an anonymous narrator.

Some readers questioned whether Hinton was losing touch with what it felt like to be a teenager. Otherwise, why would she start writing in the third person? Why wouldn't she dive in and "become" her main character, as she had in the past? But it turns out that getting older didn't have much to do with her decision. Being a mother did. Nicholas was four years old when Hinton began writing her fifth book, and four-years-olds demand a lot of energy and attention. In a Q&A for the Random House website, Hinton explained, "I was so involved with [my son] that I didn't have the emotional space to become a completely different person." But Hinton still wanted to write about teenagers. Shortly after the publication of *Taming the Star Runner*, Hinton was quoted in a collection of autobiographical sketches of YA authors saying, "I have kept writing about teenagers because, unlike most adults, I like them. It's an interesting time of life, chockfull of dramatic possibilities."

As Hinton looked back toward being a teenager—she was in her late thirties by this time—some of her interests and experiences began to seep into the novel. Travis is, after all, a writer. And a writer with a passion for horses. However, Hinton is careful to remind us that the novel is a work of fiction, and while she couldn't have written the novel without having had certain experiences, Travis's experiences are fiction. She does admit, though, that some of the things that happen to Travis when he sells his first book were based on real events, such as being at home with her cat when the publisher's call came.

Hinton has always been passionate about horses. On her website, Hinton lists horseback riding as one of her hobbies, adding that she has done both jumping and dressage. In *Tex*, she wrote about horses a little bit. In *Taming the Star Runner*, she got to write a lot more about them.

CONTINUING HER LEGACY

Despite the long gap between this novel and the earlier ones, and the different technique used to present its story, *Taming the Star Runner* deals with many of the same themes Hinton explored in her other books. Travis Harris is a fifteen-year-old trying to figure out how to make his way in the world. He's had his fair share of trouble, and when he nearly kills his stepfather with a fireplace poker he gets sent off to live with his uncle in the country. The country setting is a bit of a departure for Hinton, as is the presence of parental figures. (Travis has to deal with his Uncle Ken and Ken's wife, Teresa.) For the most part, though, his uncle is distant and Travis is left alone.

Enter Casey Kincaid, an eighteen-year-old horse trainer who rents a barn on Travis's uncle's property. She's one of Hinton's most convincing and interesting female characters, and her relationship with Travis makes up a large part of the book. Casey is trying to tame the Star Runner, the horse after whom the book is named.

Over the course of her five YA novels, Hinton constantly challenged herself to go further. *Taming the Star Runner* was no exception. Hinton's fifth book was clearly more mature than her previous novels. There are realistic relationships with parents, fully formed characters (both male and female), and several themes at play. Yet for all the maturity her writing gained over the years, Hinton never lost touch with one central thing: how it feels to be a teenager.

Some reviewers were frustrated by Travis. They felt that Travis lacked the go-get-'em approach of Hinton's other main characters. "On the surface, this fifteen-year-old resembles the classic misfits from the author's previous books; however, Track lacks Tex's zest for living," wrote Charlene Strickland in the *School Library Journal*. Other reviewers praised the book, many of them noting that they

THE OUTSIDERS HITS THE SMALL SCREEN, TOO

In March 1990, in between publishing her fifth novel, *Taming the Star Runner*, and Hinton's next writing endeavor, fans of Hinton's big screen adventures got a treat when *The Outsiders* was adapted into a television series. Directed by Francis Ford Coppola, the director behind both *The Outsiders* full-length feature and *Rumble Fish*, the TV series picked up where the movie ended. It continued the tales of the Greasers' lives after the events of *The Outsiders*.

Just as she had with the film, S. E. Hinton guided the screenwriting process, giving it more authenticity than an adaptation made by other television writers would have had. The thirteen-episode series gave Hinton the opportunity to expand immensely on many of the characters' storylines, providing depth and more elaborate stories than were given in the book or film.

The series debuted on Fox in late March 1990 — more than fourteen million viewers tuned in to the pilot—and ran through July of that year, with high ratings. But it almost never happened! A March 1990 article in the *L.A. Times* noted, "Before getting the green light at Fox two years ago, *The Outsiders* was turned down by the three major networks." The idea was kept on the back burner until Fox saw it as a viable way to earn high ratings among teenagers. The plan worked, and many of the show's actors became television heartthrobs.

were happy to see Hinton's return to writing after so many years. Patty Campbell, in the *New York Times Book Review*, noted the change in the writer's approach: "*Taming the Star Runner* is remarkable for its drive and the wry sweetness and authenticity of its voice. Gone is the golden idealism of the earlier works, perhaps because here Ms. Hinton observes, rather than participates in the innocence of her characters." Campbell also noted the impact Hinton's new maturity might have on sales: "Because *Taming the Star Runner* is also a more mature and difficult work, it may not be as popular as the other Hinton books have continued to be with succeeding generations."

After *Taming the Star Runner* came out, Hinton's writing focus began to change. In an August 1988 *Boston Globe* article, she talked about how changes in her life were changing her writing: "I'm older and I'm a parent. I wrote my first books in innocence… My writing is changing. I'm interested in putting adults and young children in my stories." Her works that followed, as a result, were a striking departure: children's books and adult fiction. It seemed Hinton would start speaking to the two audiences she had never addressed before.

REACHING NEW AUDIENCES

After a successful string of movie productions and publishing her fifth YA novel, Hinton turned back to family life and contemplated a subject for a new novel. But no story was calling out to her to be written. However, this wasn't the same writer's block she experienced after publishing *The Outsiders*. She was writing plenty; screenplays, television scripts, and advertisements were keeping her busy. She simply wasn't interested in writing another novel. On the website for Random House publishers, she explained that she "simply didn't have a story [she] wanted to tell."

Her next projects, then, were a bit of a departure. She wrote two books for younger readers: *Big David, Little David* and *The Puppy Sister* (both published in 1995). The ideas for both books came from experiences she had with her son Nicholas, or Nick, when he was a little boy.

WRITING FOR KIDS

The idea for *Big David, Little David* came from a joke Hinton and her husband played on their son, Nicholas, when he was going to his first day of school. The book uses their real names. Nick met a boy on his first day of school whose name was David, the same name as Nick's father. This boy also had dark hair and glasses, like Nick's father. So Nick asked his father, "He's not you, is he?" And—this is where the joke comes in—his father said, "Sure, Nick, that's me. Every day I get little and go to school with you." According to Hinton, the joke "freaked Nick out."

    The Puppy Sister was also inspired by Hinton's son, Nick. Hinton has called it the most auto-biographical of all her novels. In her Q&A for the Random House website, Hinton explained, "Nick is an only child and was not an animal person. He was a bit afraid of dogs, but I was determined to get him a puppy so he could connect and share attention in the family. We got our puppy when Nick was eight, and there was so much sibling rivalry between the two that he once accused me of loving the dog more than I loved him." The novelist that she is, Hinton saw a good idea for a book about a boy and his puppy. Nick provided the twist that made the book fun. He came home one day and said to Hinton, "I wonder when she will turn into a person." The book tells the tale of a puppy who slowly turns into a human and how her family adapts.

These two books reflect a shift in focus for Hinton, from the turbulent world of teenage rebels, misfits, and gang members to the more domestic world of raising a child. Ironically, Hinton's novels, which have been almost universally praised for their gritty realism, are made-up stories, and her two children's books, both of them somewhat weird and fantastic, are based on real-life events.

TURNING TOWARD HER PEERS

After a string of successful YA novels and two illustrated books geared toward young readers, few would have anticipated Hinton's next career move: fiction for adults. But that's exactly what Hinton delivered. Her next efforts were strange, but they did bear some resemblance to Hinton's prior work. Published in 2005, *Hawkes Harbor* is the tale of an illegitimate orphan, Jamie Sommers, who believes

After a nearly decade-long absence from the literary scene, Hinton returned in 2004 with her sixth novel, *Hawkes Harbor*. Unlike her classic young adult efforts, this work of adult fiction delved into the paranormal, prominently featuring a vampire as a plot element.

he has no future. Growing up in the Bronx, Catholic nuns repeatedly tell Jamie that he is fated to repeat the sins of his parents. Jamie proves them right. He takes to the sea and travels the world, becoming a smuggler, a gunrunner, and a murderer. It is a quaint seaside Delaware town, however, where Jamie encounters Grenville Hawkes, a vampire, who becomes Jamie's protector.

The plot of *Hawkes Harbor* sounds implausible to die-hard fans of Hinton's older work. After all, the violence and crime seem to reach new levels, and the presence of a vampire clearly defies Hinton's previous adhesion to realism.

OUTLIVING *THE OUTSIDERS'* LEGACY

Of all her works, *The Outsiders* remains S. E. Hinton's most widely recognized achievement. Its timeless values and the raw, gritty details that drive its plot have made it a favorite among successive generations of young adult readers. In fact, a large part of its early success came because students who hated reading simply couldn't put the book down—and their teachers noticed!

Hinton acknowledges that particular book's lasting hold, and she doesn't mind it. In August 2011, the film adaptation of *The Outsiders* was released on DVD. Hinton and several of the actors who starred in the film appeared at the premiere. In 2012, Hinton spoke at a luncheon in New York to announce *The Outsiders*' release as an ebook. In a NewsOK.com article about the luncheon, Hinton was quoted as saying, "I'll always be known for *The Outsiders*. That's easy to live with. Not many writers have an *Outsiders*, whether it's their first book or their twelfth book."

Despite her success with young adult fiction, Hinton has moved on to writing for adults, and she says she's done with the YA genre. In the aforementioned NewsOK.com article, Hinton shared, "I found that a lot of people expect me to write [*The Outsiders*] again. I can't and I don't want to. I'm proud of it and I'm glad that it's done so much good, but it's freed me up to write different things." Hinton has proven true to these words with the later works she's produced—all of which depart greatly from the content of *The Outsiders*.

On August 13, 2011, *The Outsiders* was released on DVD. At the launch party, actors Ralph Macchio (*left*) and C. Thomas Howell (*right*), who starred in the film, stand on either side of Hinton.

However, like her Oklahoma-based young adult works, *Hawkes Harbor* narrates the story of a male underdog rebel with a heart of gold. Much of Jamie's bad luck has to do with his lot in life, much like classic Hinton narrators such as Ponyboy Curtis and Tex. Reactions were mixed. The book was panned by many critics as anticlimactic and illogical. *The Washington Post* called it "a rambling episodic mess." Others praised its dramatic plot and character development.

True to form, Hinton's next effort represented another departure from form. In 2007, Hinton published a series of short stories titled *Some of Tim's Stories*. Also written for adults, this collection featured fourteen very brief stories. The tales piece together episodes from the lives of two cousins, Mike and Terry. After a drug deal gone wrong, one cousin ends up in prison and the other becomes a fugitive in Oklahoma, working at a bar. Many critics noted the brevity of the stories—some were only three or four pages! Some felt this barebones technique worked well, while others felt the stories were overshadowed by a lengthy interview published as back matter. In the latter, Hinton spoke about the plot of *Some of Tim's Stories* and her career at large.

It is not surprising that Hinton's later work diverged so greatly from her early efforts. She has never been the kind of writer who follows trends

n April 2009, Hinton attended the fourteenth annual Los Angeles Times Festival of Books in Los Angeles, California. While she has departed from her YA style, Hinton oes still sign copies of her older works, as seen above.

or worries about book sales. She writes what she wants to write, and that strategy has always worked out well for her. In the beginning, she was a high school student who wanted more stories to read about high school cliques and growing up. With each book that she wrote, Hinton honed her craft more and more, producing classic films along the way. As she embraced motherhood, she wrote for young children. And after her son left for college, she wrote about her new passion: the paranormal.

In our complex world, where it is easy to jump on every new trend, Hinton has always remained true to the subjects that excite her the most. This, in itself, is an achievement, and her books, with their countless loyal readers, are a testament to Hinton's achievement.

ON S. E. HINTON

Legal name: Susan Eloise Hinton
Birth date: July 22, 1950
Birthplace: Tulsa, Oklahoma
Current residence: Tulsa, Oklahoma
First publication: *The Outsiders*, published in
    1967 by Viking Press
Marital status: David Inhofe, 1970–present
Children: Nicholas (Nick) Inhofe
High school attended: Will Rogers High School
    (Tulsa, Oklahoma)
College attended: University of Tulsa (Tulsa,
    Oklahoma)
Favorite hobbies: Horseback riding and reading
Awards: American Library Association (ALA)
    Young Adult Services Division/*School
    Library Journal* Author Achievement Award
    (1988)

ON S. E. HINTON'S WORK

The Outsiders. **New York, NY: Viking Press, 1967.**

Synopsis: *The Outsiders* brings readers into the rivalry between two feuding teenage gangs in a world without adults. On one side stand the Socs, with money, prestige, and snobby attitudes. Their enemies are the Greasers—the rough, tough outsiders. Narrated by Ponyboy Curtis, a proud Greaser, everything is business as usual until one night goes terribly wrong. In the wake of that night, Ponyboy learns a few life lessons about pain and growing up the hard way.

Awards: *New York Herald Tribune* Best Teenage Books list (1967), *Chicago Tribune Book World* Spring Book Festival Honor Book (1967), Media and Methods Maxi Award (1975), American Library Association (ALA) Best Young Adult Books citation

(1975), Massachusetts Children's Book
Award (1979)

That Was Then, This Is Now. New York, NY: Viking Press, 1971.

Synopsis: Set a few years later in the same
town as *The Outsiders*, *That Was Then...* is
the story of two best friends, Bryon and Mark,
as they grow apart. Bryon is maturing and
thinking about his future; Mark still enjoys
teenage thrills. Their relationship persists
until Bryon must make a life-altering decision
that will affect them both.

Awards: American Library Association (ALA)
Best Books for Young Adults citation (1971),
Chicago Tribune Book World Spring Book
Festival Honor Book (1971), Massachusetts
Children's Book Award (1978)

Rumble Fish. New York, NY: Delacorte Press, 1975.

Synopsis: Rusty-James is an all-around tough
guy who relies more on brawn than brains.
He idolizes his older brother, Motorcycle Boy,
and whenever he gets into trouble, Motorcycle Boy helps get him out. But
Rusty-James's lack of direction and his

ambition to be like his brother slowly wreck his world until it falls apart—and Motorcycle Boy is no longer there to come to his rescue.

Awards: American Library Association (ALA) Best Books for Young Adults citation (1975), *School Library Journal* Best Books of the Year citation (1975), New Mexico Library Association Land of Enchantment Award (1982)

***Tex*. New York, NY: Delacorte Press, 1979.**

Synopsis: With their father away on the rodeo circuit, fifteen-year-old *Tex* and his older brother Mason are left on their own to take care of their house, their horses, and the bills. But *Tex* thinks life is perfect. However, when Mason must sell off the horses—including Tex's horse, Negrito—Tex grows angry. And when Mason wants to escape Oklahoma, Tex's future becomes highly uncertain.

Awards: American Library Association (ALA) Best Books for Young Adults citation (1979), *School Library Journal* Best Books of the Year citation (1979), New York Public Library Books for the Teen-Age citation (1980), American Book Award nomination (1981), Louisiana Association of School Librarians Sue Hefley Honor Book (1982), California Reading Association's California Young

Reader Medal nomination (1982), Wisconsin Educational Media & Technology Association's Golden Archer Award (1983)

Taming the Star Runner. New York, NY: Delacorte Press, 1988.
Synopsis: Travis Harris is a troubled teen who gets sent to live with his uncle in the country. His tough city ways make him an outcast, except with Casey Kincaid, the beautiful horse trainer who rents a barn on his uncle's property. While Casey tries to tame her wild horse, Star Runner, Travis feels an affinity with the beast that can't be trained.
Awards: American Library Association (ALA) Best Books for Young Adults citation (1988), Colorado Blue Spruce Young Adult Book Award nomination (1990)

Big David, Little David, illustrated by Alan Daniel. New York, NY: Doubleday, 1995.
Synopsis: When Nick starts kindergarten, he runs into a classmate that not only looks like his father, David, but also has the same name! In this illustrated children's book, Nick must determine who is who and whether or not his father really shrinks each day to accompany him to school.

The Puppy Sister, illustrated by Jacqueline Rogers. New York, NY: Delacorte, 1995.
Synopsis: The Davidsons are a great family. Mom and Dad are friendly, and while the only child, Nick, would prefer to have a sister, he'll still play with Aleasha the puppy. Aleasha loves her family a lot, so much so that she wishes she could look like them and talk like them, too. She comes up with a plan to become a human, and Nick must quickly prepare for his new sister.

Hawkes Harbor. New York, NY: Tor Books, 2004.
Synopsis: An orphan and illegitimate, Jamie Sommers believes he has "no hope of heaven." As a Catholic, Jamie believes he is destined to repeat the sins of his parents and follows suit. He takes to the sea and works in exotic ports the world over as a smuggler, a gunrunner—and even a murderer. Jamie has seen it all, but a quiet beach town in Delaware will show him the ultimate evil. *Hawkes Harbor* will drive him insane and alter his life forever.

Some of Tim's Stories. Norman, OK: University of Oklahoma Press, 2007.
Synopsis: This collection of fourteen short stories paints concise, incisive portraits of a cast

of characters shaped by life and one another. A larger narrative emerges: that of two cousins, Mike and Terry, whose lives meet and then diverge. After a drug deal goes wrong, one cousin ends up in prison and the other becomes a fugitive, working at a bar. With the stories comes an exclusive interview with S. E. Hinton about this book and her career at large.

The Outsiders (1967)

"This remarkable novel gives a moving, credible view of *the outsiders* from the inside... we meet powerful characters in a book with a powerful message."—*Horn Book*

"At a time when the average young-adult novel was, in Hinton's characterization, 'Mary Jane went to the prom,' *The Outsiders* shocked readers with its frank depictions of adolescents smoking, drinking and 'rumbling'... Long credited with changing the way Y.A. fiction is written, Hinton's novel changed the way teenagers read as well, empowering a generation to demand stories that reflected their realities."—Dale Peck, *New York Times Sunday Book Review*

Rumble Fish (1975)

"The novel (really a novella) originated as a short story and retains the compact power of that genre. It has a small cast of characters and a simple plot. Every gesture feels essential." —Jon Michaud, *New Yorker*

"As gut-wrenching as the 'sneaky pete' her hero guzzles down, S. E. Hinton's latest novel won't sit well with book selectors who demand that children's fiction end hopefully, if not happily... Stylistically superb (the purpose-fully flat, colorless narrative exactly describes [main character] Rusty-James' turf of pool halls, porno movie houses, and seedy hang-outs), this packs a punch that will leave readers of any age reeling."—Jane Abramson, *School Library Journal*

Tex (1979)

"Hinton's style has matured since she exploded on to the YA scene in 1967 with *The Outsiders* (Viking). In *Tex*, the raw energy for which Hinton has justifiably reaped praise has not been tamed—it's been cultivated, and the result is a fine, solidly constructed and well-paced story... Personal discoveries emerge from the action in a natural, unpretentious, and nondidactic way as Hinton explores questions about responsibility, friendship, desire, and communication."—Marilyn Kaye, *School Library Journal*

Taming the Star Runner (1988)

"Devoted fans will leap on Hinton's new novel, yet her protagonist Travis is no Tex (Delacorte, 1979). On the surface, this fifteen-year-old resembles the classic misfits from the author's previous books; however, Travis lacks Tex's zest for living... Hinton builds a sparse plot

around a predominately bleak theme.
Although the story isn't fleshed out, tough-
guy Travis will appeal to a certain readership.
Others will find him forgettable, especially
compared to his fictional predecessors."
—Charlene Strickland, *School Library Journal*

Big David, Little David (1995)
"Exuberant mixed-medium illustrations, rich in
watercolor and delightful details, will capti-
vate children. The warm fuzzy family story
definitely has charm and abounds with clever
humor that's sure to tickle adults and may
delight gifted children, but it's likely to baffle
most kids."—Jody McCoy, *School Library
Journal*

"Considerably less reassuring than the usual first-
day-of-kindergarten fare, this offbeat picture
book has a certain ambiguity that might make
preschoolers uncomfortable. Slightly older
children, though, will probably enjoy the story.
The colorful illustrations, featuring well-drawn
characters and comical situations, will have
broad appeal."—Carolyn Phelan, *Booklist*

The Puppy Sister (1995)
"With this whimsical animal story, Hinton serves

up an entry as memorable in its genre as her classic *The Outsiders* is in YA literature... Offering a unique, consistently witty account of growing pains and family life, this irresistible fantasy can take its place alongside Stuart Little and Babe the Gallant Pig."
—*Publishers Weekly*

Hawkes Harbor (2004)

"The story line veers from gothic melodrama to Munstersish family comedy when the cursed bloodsucker regains his mortality and settles into a perversely fatherly relationship with the now-addled Jamie. As startling as this story line may sound, Hinton manages to work in quite a few clichés (stakes through the heart, keening virgins, etc.), and sentimentality frequently wells up alongside the elements of parody."—Jennifer Mattson, *Booklist*

"Hinton knows how to tell a story, and this one's entertaining, ghoulish, and full of fantastical adventures. But the non-chronological time frame and confusing narration left some reviewers bewildered. A few unexplained elements, from Jamie's fading voice and changes in Hawkes's personality, also left them hanging. But, if you're curious to know what Hinton's been up to the past 25 years and don't expect a classic, *Hawkes Harbor* is worth a go."—*Bookmarks Magazine*

Some of Tim's Stories (2007)

"…Readers curious about a beloved writer's mature output won't want to skip the novella, aimed at an adult audience, where linked vignettes about male cousins form a smooth continuum with Hinton's gritty, guy-dominated YA novels."—Jennifer Mattson, *Booklist*

1950: Born July 22, in Tulsa, Oklahoma.

1967: *The Outsiders* is published.

1968: "Rumble Fish," a short story, is published in *Nimrod* magazine, the literary supplement to the *University of Tulsa Alumni Magazine.*

1970: Hinton receives bachelor of science degree from the University of Tulsa, majoring in education; she marries David Inhofe.

1971: *That Was Then, This Is Now* is published.

1975: *Rumble Fish* is published as a novel.

1979: *Tex* is published.

1980: Hinton sells film rights for *The Outsiders* (to Zoetrope Studios) and *Tex* (to Disney Studios).

1982: *Tex*, the movie, is released in September.

1983: Hinton's son, Nicholas David Inhofe, is born in August. The movie version of *The Outsiders* is released in March, followed by *Rumble Fish*, which is released in October.

1985: *That Was Then, This Is Now*, the movie, is released in November.

1988: *Taming the Star Runner* is published; Hinton receives the first ever Author Achievement Award from the Young Adult Services Division of the American Library Association and *School Library Journal.*

TIMELINE

1990: *The Outsiders* is adapted as a play by playwright Christopher Sergel and as a television series by Francis Ford Coppola.

1995: Hinton publishes two children's books: *Big David, Little David* and *The Puppy Sister.*

2004: *Hawkes Harbor* is published.

2007: *Some of Tim's Stories* is published.

2009: Hinton makes a cameo in the film *Legend of Billy Fail.*

2011: Hinton has an uncredited appearance in an episode of the television series *Supernatural.*

ADAPTATION The re-creation and transfer of a story to a new medium.

ARTICULATE Expressing oneself clearly.

CAMARADERIE Good will among friends; light-hearted friendship.

CAMEO A small role, played by someone famous.

CLICHÉ An idea or phrase that is no longer interesting because it's been used too much.

CLIQUE A small, exclusive group of friends.

COMPROMISE To settle for something by giving something else up.

DELINQUENT A person who breaks the law or fails to follow the rules.

DRESSAGE A type of riding in which the rider guides his or her horse through a series of maneuvers.

EMPATHY The ability to share another's thoughts, emotions, or feelings.

ILLEGITIMATE Born out of wedlock.

IRONIC Opposite to what is or might be expected.

MOTIVATION Something that drives someone to action.

NARRATOR The character who tells a story.

PHENOMENON An unusual or remarkable fact or occurrence.

PREVAIL To be widespread or common.

PROSE Ordinary writing, without poetic structure.

RIVAL A competitor.

ROYALTIES The share of the money made from a book's sales that are paid to the author.

SENSATIONALIST Using shock, horror, or exaggeration to get a reaction.

SENTIMENTAL Playing on one's emotions to get a response.

SIBLING RIVALRY Competition between brothers and/or sisters.

WRITER'S BLOCK A usually temporary condition in which a writer finds himself or herself unable to write.

Canadian Library Association (CLA)
1150 Morrison Drive, Suite 400
Ottawa, ON K2H 8S9
Canada
(613) 232-9625
Website: https://www.cla.ca
The CLA is the premier organization in Canada
devoted to promoting the interests of libraries
and pushing for informed public policies that
promote literacy and book research. Its CLA
Young Adult Book Award recognizes top
English-language Canadian publications for
young adults each year.

Curtis Brown, Ltd.
Attn: S. E. Hinton
Ten Astor Place
New York, NY 10003
(212) 473-5400
Email: info@cbltd.com
Website: http://www.curtisbrown.com
Since the publication of *The Outsiders*, Curtis Brown,
Ltd. has represented S. E. Hinton as the author's
agent. They have information on the rights,
permissions, publications, and awards given to
Hinton's various works and film adaptations.

Dramatic Publishing
311 Washington Street
Woodstock, IL 60098
(800) 448-7469
Website: http://www.dramaticpublishing.com/p1128/
    The-Outsiders/product_info.html
Dramatic Publishing is the publisher responsible for
    Christopher Sergel's play adaptation of *The
    Outsiders*. It sells rights, scripts, and sound
    effects to those interested in producing the
    classic Hinton tale.

School Library Journal (SLJ)
123 William Street, Suite 802
New York, NY 10038
(646) 380-0700
Website: http://slj.com
SLJ is a major hub of young adult and children's
    publishing, promoting the information, literacy,
    and technology needs of students and libraries
    everywhere. It publishes reviews of YA books,
    such as those of S. E. Hinton.

Society of Children's Book Writers & Illustrators
    (SCBWI)
8271 Beverly Boulevard
Los Angeles, CA 90048
(323) 782-1010
Website: http://www.scbwi.org

The Society of Children's Book Writers & Illustrators is an organization for writers and illustrators of children's and young adult literature. The group has chapters around the world where members can share ideas, information, and tips about writing children's literature.

Young Adult Library Services Association (YALSA)
50 East Huron Street
Chicago, IL 60611
(800) 545-2433
Website: http://www.ala.org/yalsa
YALSA is the division of the American Library Association (ALA) dedicated to promoting young adult literature. It gives annual awards for YA books and provides resources to students who have a passion for reading.

WEBSITES

Because of the changing nature of Internet links, Rosen Publishing has developed an online list of websites related to the subject of this book. This site is updated regularly. Please use this link to access this list:

http://www.rosenlinks.com/AAA/Hinton

Abrams, Dennis. *S. E. Hinton* (Who Wrote That?). New York, NY: Chelsea House, 2009.

Daly, Jay. *Presenting S. E. Hinton*. Boston, MA: Twayne Publishers, 1987.

Donald R. Gallo, ed. *Speaking for Ourselves: Autobiographical Sketches by Notable Authors of Books for Young Adults*. Urbana, IL: National Council of Teachers of English, 1990.

Harmon, Daniel E. *Cassandra Clare* (All About the Author). New York, NY: Rosen Publishing, 2015.

Hinton, S. E. *Big David, Little David*, illustrated by Alan Daniel. New York, NY: Doubleday, 1995.

Hinton, S. E. *Hawkes Harbor*. New York, NY: Tor Books, 2004.

Hinton, S. E. *Rumble Fish*. New York, NY: Delacorte Press, 1975.

Hinton, S. E. *Some of Tim's Stories*. Norman, OK: University of Oklahoma Press, 2007.

Hinton, S. E. *Taming the Star Runner*. New York, NY: Delacorte Press, 1988.

Hinton, S. E. *Tex*. New York, NY: Delacorte Press, 1979.

Hinton, S. E. *That Was Then, This Is Now*. New York, NY: Viking Press, 1971.

Hinton, S. E. *The Outsiders*. New York, NY: Viking Press, 1967.

Hinton, S. E. *The Puppy Sister*, illustrated by Jacqueline Rogers. New York, NY: Delacorte, 1995.

Joubert, Sarah. *The Outsiders* by S. E. Hinton (Literature Kit). San Diego, CA: Classroom Complete Press, 2013.

Kamberg, Mary-Lane. *Margaret Peterson Haddix* (All About the Author). New York, NY: Rosen Publishing, 2014.

Kjelle, Marylou Morano. *S. E. Hinton: Author of The Outsiders* (Authors Teens Love). Berkeley Heights, NJ: Enslow Publishers, 2008.

Nelson, David E. *Teen Issues in S.E. Hinton's The Outsiders* (Social Issues in Literature). Detroit, MI: Greenhaven Press, 2012.

Niver, Heather Moore. *Veronica Roth* (All About the Author). New York, NY: Rosen Publishing, 2015.

Poolos, Christine. *John Green* (All About the Author). New York, NY: Rosen Publishing, 2015.

Staley, Erin. *Maggie Stiefvater* (All About the Author). New York, NY: Rosen Publishing, 2014.

Wolny, Philip. *James Dashner* (All About the Author). New York, NY: Rosen Publishing, 2014.

Andrews, Sheryl. "Review of *That Was Then, This Is Now.*" *Horn Book*, July–August 1971, p. 338.

"Biography." SEHinton.com. Retrieved July 6, 2015 (http://sehinton.com/bio.html).

Campbell, Patty. "Review of *Taming the Star Runner.*" *New York Times Book Review*, April 2, 1989, p. 26.

Campbell, Patty. "The Young Adult Perplex." *Wilson Library Bulletin*, September 1985, p. 62.

Cart, Michael. "Review of *That Was Then, This Is Now.*" *New York Times Book Review*, August 8, 1971, p. 8.

Daly, Jay. *Presenting S. E. Hinton*. Boston, MA: Twayne Publishers, 1989.

de Montreville, Doris, and Elizabeth D. Crawford, eds. *Fourth Book of Junior Authors*. New York, NY: H.W. Wilson Co., 1978.

Ehrichs, Lisa. "Advice from a Penwoman." *Seventeen*, Vol. 40, November 1981, p.32.

"Face to Face with a Teen-Age Novelist." *Seventeen*. October 1967.

Farber, Stephen. "Directors Join the S.E. Hinton Fan Club." *New York Times,* March 20, 1983. Retrieved July 8, 2015 (http://www.nytimes.com/1983/03/20/movies/directors-join-the-se-hinton-fan-club.html).

Fisher, Margery. "Review of Tex." *Growing Point*, May 1980, pp. 3686-87.

Fisher, Margery. "Review of *Rumble Fish.*" *Growing*

Point, May 1976, p. 2894.

Fleming, Thomas. "Review of *The Outsiders*." *New York Times Book Review*, May 7, 1967. Retrieved July 8, 2015 (http://query.nytimes.com/gst/abstract.html?res=980CE2D71F3 CE53BBC4F53DFB366838C679EDE).

Harmetz, Aljean. "Making *The Outsiders*, a Librarian's Dream." *New York Times*, March 23, 1983. Retrieved July 8, 2015 (http://www.nytimes.com/1983/03/23/movies/making-the-outsiders-a-librarian-s-dream.html).

Hentoff, Nat. "Review of *The Outsiders*." *Atlantic Monthly*, December 1967.

Hinton, Hal. "Writer of *Tex* Is Comfortable Dealing with Disney and Coppola." *Chicago Tribune*, December 24, 1982. Retrieved July 8, 2015 (http://archives.chicagotribune.com/1982/12/24/page/47/article/movies).

Hinton, Susan. "Teen-Agers Are for Real." *New York Times Book Review*, August 27, 1967. Retrieved July 8, 2015 (http://query.nytimes.com/gst/abstract.html?res=9E06E4D81039 E530A25754C2A96E9C946691D6CF).

Hinton, S.E. "S.E. Hinton: On Writing and Tex." *Notes from Delacorte Press for Books for Young Readers*, Issue 406, Winter 1979/Spring 1980. New York, NY: Delacorte Press.

Kaye, Marilyn. "Review of Tex." *School Library*

Journal. November 1979.

Loer, Stephanie. "Bringing Realism to Teen-Age Fiction." *Boston Globe*, August 31, 1988.

Litchfield, Yvonne. "Her Book to Be Published Soon, but Tulsa Teen-Ager Keeps Cool." *Tulsa Daily World*, April 7, 1967.

Michaud, Jon. "*That Was Then, This Is Now*: S. E. Hinton in the Twitter Age." *New Yorker*, November 8, 2013. Retrieved July 8, 2015 (http://www.newyorker.com/books/page-turner/that-was-then-this-is-now-s-e-hinton-in-the-twitter-age).

Peck, Dale. "*The Outsiders*: 40 Years Later." *New York Times*, September 23, 2007. Retrieved July 8, 2015 (http://www.nytimes.com/2007/09/23/books/review/Peck-t.html).

Powell, Jane. "Urban Guerrillas." *Times Literary Supplement*, April 2, 1976.

"Review of *Rumble Fish*." *Kirkus Review*, October 15, 1975. Retrieved July 6, 2015 (https://www.kirkusreviews.com/book-reviews/se-hinton/rumble-fish).

"Review of *Rumble Fish*." *Publisher's Weekly*, Issue 208, July 28, 1975.

Scott, Jay. "Susie Loves Matt." *American Film*, Vol. VIII, No. 6, April 1983, pp. 34–35.

"S. E. Hinton." Penguin Random House. Retrieved July 6, 2015 (http://www.penguinrandomhouse.com/authors/13074/se-hinton).

Smith, Dave. "Hinton: What Boys Are Made Of."
Los Angeles Times, July 15, 1982.

Strickland, Charlene. "Review of *Taming the Star Runner*." *School Library Journal*, Vol. 35, No. 2, October 1988.

Sutherland, Zena. "The Teen-Ager Speaks." *Saturday Review*, January 27, 1968.

Tipping, Joy. "S. E. Hinton on How *The Outsiders* Worked Its Way into the Mainstream." *Dallas Morning News*, April 18, 2014, Retrieved July 9, 2015 (http://www.dallasnews. com/lifestyles/books/20140418-s.e.-hinton- on-how-the-outsiders-worked-its-way-into- the-mainstream.ece).

V

Viking Press, 10
violence, 20

W

Will Rogers High School, 9

Y

YASD/SLJ Margaret A.
    Edwards Award, 65, 67
young adult (YA) fiction, 6,
    8, 65, 67, 73, 75, 78

ABOUT THE AUTHOR

Joseph Franklin is a YA author who first read *The Outsiders* in middle school. Aside from being an S. E. Hinton fan, he loves reading, writing, and walking his dog, Bucky.

Antoine Wilson is the author of *The Young Zillionaire's Guide to Distributing Goods and Services*, *Family Matters: You and a Death in Your Family*, and *The Assassination of President McKinley*. He lives in Southern California.

PHOTO CREDITS

Designer: Nicole Russo; Editor: Jacob Steinberg; Photo Researcher: Nicole DiMella